THE SEA IS SINGING

THE SEA IS SINGING

A. K. Johnson

ISBN: 978-9988-3-4138-1

Published by Aspire Publishing Limited.
No.21 General Carl Modey Street, Adjiriganor, Accra
P.O Box AN 18720 Accra-North
Tel: 0302-508848/0244815649
info@aspirepublishing.com.gh
www. aspirepublishing.com.gh

Cover Illustration by Minds2ink studio
Cover Design and Page Layout by Sam Nyarko-Mensah

CONTENTS

1

PIZZA

Bigboy, known by his friends as BB, was stout, with scruffy sideburns on a big, square head. He was in glowing spirits that cloudy Monday morning. Swiping the face of his latest smart phone, he called, "What's up, guys? Why are you guys so late? I've been hanging around the mall for the past two hours."

While waiting, Bigboy bought some popcorn and stood in front of a display window of a boutique. Soon, Joe and Slim joined him.

Bigboy glanced at Joe for some seconds and smiled. "Are you in this pink shirt again, Joe? I've noticed that you don't groom well at all. Look at the stains on your shirt. You've not even combed your hair properly. You need to spruce up and be cute."

"BB, you're fond of talking about clothes all the time. I know how to shape up, but the problem is the cash. If I get the cash, I'll be the best dressed person in town."

Slim muffled a giggle, which made Bigboy look at him in a repulsive way. "Slim, why are you laughing at Joe? When it comes to grooming, you're worse than Joe. Today, I must teach the two of you about good grooming. I feel bad walking with guys like you. Look at Slim! You're always in this long gown and skull cap. C'mon, you guys need to spruce up."

"Why are you tongue-lashing us this morning, BB?" Joe interrupted.

Joe and Slim, "I invited you today so that we can do some shopping. I've landed on some cash. "

"Hmnn! Let's get to the restaurant and blow it up." Slim smiled and rubbed his palms together in excitement. "I'm hungry."

"Slim, you're always for food. You live to eat. Let's check some new jeans in that shop." Bigboy took the lead.

"I don't have any money, so I only window-shop." Joe whispered.

"I can't afford to shop in boutiques." Slim protested.

"C'mon, let's get into this shop. I'm prepared to sponsor you."

"Are you sure, BB?" Joe exclaimed.

"Just follow me."

Joe picked up the jeans and looked at the manufacturer's label. "Are they original jeans?"

"Very original," replied the smiling salesgirl.

"I don't like the finish of the back pockets," Bigboy said, shaking his head.

"It's the latest fashion," replied the salesgirl. "It's moving fast. We brought in five hundred two weeks ago and only eighty are left. I'm sure by the end of the week everything will be snapped up."

"I wear size thirty," Joe was excited.

"Let me fit into size twenty-six," Slim said.

Bigboy was surprised. "Slim, you have a mosquito waist. I wear thirty-eight. My problem is the length. I'm short, so I must reduce the length."

"BB, you're round like a barrel," Joe chuckled.

"Stop that, Joe," Bigboy said, removing his wallet. "I want each of you to pick one quality pair of jeans, a T-shirt, a cap, a sunshade, and sneakers."

"Eh! Can you afford it?" Joe asked.

"Money is not my problem, but how to spend it. My dad returned from Europe last night and gave me a lot of money to spend. As classmates, I want to spend it with you. What are friends for?"

Slim was excited and continued rubbing his palms together. "Sssh! I wish you could convert mine into cash for me. The jeans are too expensive in this shop. This designer T-shirt and sneakers can feed me for months."

"Shut up, Slim! It's my dough, so I decide how it should be spent. I'm not happy with the way you look when you're with me. I'm always in the latest fashion and stand out as trendy. I feel uncomfortable amongst you, so I want you to catch up with me."

"OK, BB. We'll make the choice, and you pay. " Joe also rubbed his palms gleefully. For hours, they romped through the boutiques at the mall, shopping for the latest designer brands.

Bigboy was thrilled; he led Joe and Slim to the washroom to change into their new clothes at once.

The next moment, the boys came out, glittering in their latest look. Bigboy was pleased with his handiwork and patted Joe fondly on the shoulder. "Yeah! Big Joe! You look like a modern guy now. From now, you should be able to walk up to a lady and propose. Now I'll be proud when you go with me to meet the black beauty. I've been tracking her for some time now."

"I know it's our classmate Genevieve," Slim blurted.

"Keep quiet! It's my secret. You'll know her one day." Bigboy whispered. "Slim, do you see how Joe is looking fresh and modern?"

Suddenly, Joe was inflated with pride and flashed the thumbs-up sign, rubbing his palms briskly together as they walked towards the restaurant. To their utter amazement, Bigboy stopped abruptly. "I don't like the way you guys are walking like some rural bush boys. You must walk like this to prove that you are tough guys in town. I want my girlfriend to know that my friends are the latest guys in town. Look at me. Look at the way I walk and copy it now."

Bigboy swaggered up and down as Joe and Slim cheered. Soon the three boys were swaggering down the mall. When Bigboy was satisfied with their walk, he grinned with pleasure. "I want to give you guys a treat for your neat appearance. Let's go and eat some pizza and some drinks, then to the cinema. Today's movie is a rollercoaster that takes one high and low. It was premiered last week and it's the talk on all the radio, television stations and the social media."

"BB, pizza is too light for me," Slim mumbled. "If I can get some *banku*, hot pepper, and fried fish to fill me for the full day, I'll be pleased. We can save a lot if we eat roasted plantains and groundnuts." Slim added.

"There goes Slim again! You're always saving money, always trying to save units on your mobile phone. Don't worry; I'll pay for the pizza. You have everything on me. Guys, you must eat sophisticated food when you're in expensive jeans and sneakers. Why go local when you're in the latest, trendy clothes?" Bigboy ruled.

The three boys enjoyed their pizza and drinks and went to the cinema afterwards.

When the movie was over, Bigboy led his squad to the popcorn joint and ordered three buckets. "Guys, I did not enjoy the movie at all. The ad was overblown."

"BB, it was a very interesting movie. I'll watch it a thousand times," said Slim. "You know, BB slept for more than an hour. How can he appreciate a movie while snoring? You must come again to watch it while wide awake. Joe, what are your comments about the movie?"

"A great movie! The love scene was fantastic. . ."

"There goes Mr. Lover man. Reducing everything in the world to love," Bigboy said. "BB, love makes the world go round." Slim stressed.

"But at times, love brings the world to a standstill," Bigboy looked at Slim with a wry smile on his face.

2

WAAKYE

When he was with his friends, his nickname was Slim. At home, he was called Yakubu. Bigboy coined the name "Slim" and since then, it has been the name they used. Slim meandered his way through the dark alleys of Sokora. He had to be alert because he did not trust the area boys who tormented people in the township. The other day, a boy who pretended to be a beggar snatched his mobile phone. Slim gave him a hot chase until the miscreant threw the phone into a drain and dissolved into the darkness.

On many occasions, Slim's parents had warned him to be home early to help with some of the chores, but Slim had defied them. His hobby was to hang out with friends at shopping malls in the city.

"Yakubu, you're late again. I've advised you for years. I'll not warn you again. I'm an experienced person. " Baba warned.

"I went to study, and the traffic was heavy today."

As Slim ate his supper, his mind drifted to the shopping mall where Bigboy bought clothes and pizza for them. Suddenly, he had realised that the pizza was tastier and more expensive than the dry *waakye* and *wele*, which were in front of him on the three-legged table. He fetched some spoonful of the *waakye* and looked at the flickering candle, which would go off at any moment. The *wele* was like a piece of rubber, and as Slim tried and tried to chew it, it sprang out of his mouth onto the floor.

The candle was fluttering and crackling, a sign that it was at its end. The tongue of the flame leapt high for the last time and crashed into the wax, plunging the room into darkness. It was the last candle that had held the fort since the pre-paid electricity metre went off.

Slim was seventeen years old and had not understood Baba, his father, an experienced plumber who worked in the Public Works Department. He had nine children with three women. Slim was very angry to learn that his father was preparing to marry a fourth wife. For days, he had been battling with the idea of confronting his father to stop the marriage. One day, he gathered courage and knocked on the door. "Baba, I want to see you."

"Yakubu, I hope it's not about the school fees. Of late I've been busy with some other things. I'll settle the last examination fees at the end of this month," he smiled.

"Baba, it's not the fees. I've heard rumours that you're... you're...er...er...going to marry again."

"It's not a rumour. It's a fact. The ceremony is in two weeks' time. I've spent money buying things for the occasion."

"Baba, but er---er---you have many children already and looking after us is a problem."

"You're a child. Don't I look after you? Are you not housed, clothed, and fed? It's not a problem at all. My elder brother Mustafa has sixteen children."

"Baba, you know that my uncle Mustafa is suffering. Look at his children, who are mostly school dropouts..."

"Shut up! Yakubu. Just leave the room."

Slim saw the wave of angry ripples surging on his father's face and jumped out. He had known his father for his mood swings. One moment, he was the happiest person, and the next moment, he was in a temper.

Slim stood on the veranda, musing over what his father had just said. He was amazed that his father was proud of the housing, the clothing, and the food. Sadly, every morning it was *koko* and bread or *koose*. Lunch was never provided at home. Usually, supper was *waakye* or *tuozafi*, and as for clothing, Slim recalled that his mother was the one who bought second-hand clothes for him.

Slim's mobile phone screeched early that Thursday morning. "What's up, BB?" Slim listened carefully and smiled. "BB, I'll be there Saturday sharp."

3

KENKEY AND FISH

Genevieve was in her red blouse and blue jeans again. She liked the colour red. No wonder many of her friends called her "the lady in red." But Genevieve had her own reason for wearing the red blouse. If she looked in her wardrobe, it was the newest and most modern thing that fit her. Most of her clothes were ill-fitting tie-dyed long, cotton frocks until Esi, her classmate, went on vacation and brought her the jeans and blouse. Genevieve had not forgotten that wonderful gift. On many occasions, Genevieve wondered how she met Esi in school that day when they sat next to each other in class.

At first, Esi did not look at Genevieve at all. She looked straight ahead and did not even want her uniform to touch Genevieve's. During the morning break, Esi was aloof and stood under a tree reading comics and eating yoghurt. Genevieve feared Esi's bluff, but she decided to walk towards her. "Hello! I didn't introduce myself to you earlier. My name is Genevieve."

"I'm Esi."

"Have a piece of bread..."

Esi refused angrily and walked away. Genevieve, sagging with shame and embarrassment, felt the earth swallow her. The piece of bread fell from her hands and tears loaded her eyes.

Genevieve was so hurt in class that day that she did not answer any questions. After school, as she prepared to walk to the *tro-tro* station, Esi's mother came to pick her up in a sleek Mercedes Benz car. Genevieve shivered and suddenly felt that Esi was in a special class of her own. Even on the rattling *tro-tro* back home, Genevieve still thought of Esi as a girl from an affluent home.

Esi had shrugged off Genevieve the whole term until something remarkable happened when the results of the first term were published, and the student who came out with distinction was Genevieve. She topped all the subjects, and all the teachers praised her. It was at this point that Esi became warm towards Genevieve, who was willing to solve all the complex mathematics problems and explain all the scientific concepts easily to her mates.

For some time, Esi wanted to know more about the brilliant girl who topped the class. When Esi asked Genevieve about the background of her parents, she panicked and did not show it for days. Then one day, Genevieve told Esi that her father was the captain of a ship and her mother a caterer. Genevieve felt relieved with some pride and noticed the respect Esi had for her.

Not long afterwards, Genevieve was surprised one day when Esi brought her a small parcel, which had the blue jeans and red blouse. The gift shocked Genevieve the entire day, and she thought she was dreaming. It was at that moment that Esi also disclosed a lot about herself to Genevieve.

Esi was the only daughter of Mr. James Ansah and Mrs. Eleanor Ansah. Mr. Ansah was a hard-working accountant who died tragically in a car crash. As a result, Mrs. Ansah inherited a huge, landed property from her deceased husband. Unfortunately, Mrs. Ansah, in her desire to make more money, started gambling at casinos. The family's fortune eroded, but Mrs. Ansah continued gambling, which led to a heavy loss. The habit made Mrs. Ansah irritable, depressed, and reserved. Esi was heavily affected by her mother's neglect, so it was not strange that she chose Genevieve as a friend to lean on.

One day, when Mrs. Ansah returned home heavily drunk, Esi was so embarrassed that she decided to flee to seek her freedom by visiting Genevieve at the weekend.

Genevieve lived in Shorkor, an inner city of the capital town. Esi's planned visit made her so nervous that she had sleepless nights. Genevieve cleaned their little room, which faced the sea. Then she went to another friend's house and arranged for a television set to be placed in their tiny sitting room.

Just as she was fixing the curtains, her father called, "Are you in the room, Ayorkor?"

"Yes, papa. I'm still busy doing some cleaning."

"Come out and meet your friend, she called you by a name we're not familiar with. Genevieve---er---when did you add that to your name?"

Genevieve's feet trembled as she stepped out of the room. Immediately she saw Esi, her face nearly dropped to the ground. Esi sat on the torn sofa and scanned the room. In the far corner was a spider dangling in its web, then a wall gecko scuttled on the windowsill and dropped on the bare floor. Esi tried to switch on the television set, but the reception was blurred. A little radio on a table blared out music. There was no refrigerator in the room; Esi had to buy bottled water from a shop nearby. For a long time, Genevieve ran around like a little chicken trying to please Esi, who was also wondering whether she was in the right house or daydreaming. At last, Esi broke the silence. "Your father just told me he's a fisherman. Why did you introduce him as a captain of a ship?"

Genevieve's face was heavy with guilt. "I'm sorry to deceive you. I did that to tickle my pride. I felt you didn't respect me, so I had to tell you, so you don't look down on me."

"But you should have told me the truth."

"Would you have respected me if you had known I was from a poor home?"

Esi could not answer; she stared at Genevieve and said, "It's better to speak the truth and be free. Be proud of what you have instead of copying others. Do you know why I'm here?"

"Of course, to visit me."

"I'm not a happy child despite the riches. My house is falling apart, and I'll love a house where my parents take an interest in what I'm doing. I've left home to cool down for the night. I want to be with you till tomorrow."

"Will you be happy in this small place? We don't have many amenities."

"I'll be happy."

There was a knock on the door, and Genevieve's mother entered. She was a vivacious woman who electrified the room with her pleasant smile. "You're welcome, Esi. I'm a *kenkey* and fish seller. I'll give you some to eat."

Quickly, she arranged for some food for the children. Genevieve's father also joined them and was eager to know more about Esi. It was a very exciting day for Esi to be chatting and laughing for hours. She had missed parental love over the years.

Esi experienced the reality of life in Shorkor, which was another part of the city. For the first time in her life, she slept on a mat without a pillow, queued to pay for water to have her bath in the morning, and ate without using a fork and knife.

Esi enjoyed her brief stay at Shorkor; she kept wondering how Genevieve was able to manage it in such a place to be the star of the class.

4

THE SCORPION

That Saturday morning, Bigboy, Slim and Joe were at the Oxford Street, a popular busy suburb of the capital. The suburb hosts many of the popular food joints and businesses. It was sunny so they wore their sunshades and entered one of the food joints to have lunch. Bigboy belched and licked his fingers as he finished the last piece of his chicken.

Slim's cheeks were smeared with oil because of the way he wolfed down the chicken and continuously smacked his lips. Bigboy enjoyed such occasions when he led his friends to shopping centres and bought food for them. He was a voracious eater and was always the first to finish his meal. Sometimes he enjoyed observing Slim chewing his meat carefully and Joe belching in-between meals. Bigboy always felt he was the donor, the planner, and the source of ideas. After the meals, Bigboy rammed the table. "Guys, I want us to do something new today."

"What's it?" Slim exclaimed.

"It's a top secret. You just follow me." Bigboy waddled ahead whilst the rest followed him timidly. They jumped into a taxi and made their way towards the central business centre and snaked through kiosks and containers until they entered a shack. A wiry man in a dreadlocks hairstyle and a goatee beard squeezed a smile out of his bony face. "I've been waiting for you since morning, Bigboy."

"Hey! Rastafarian, Haile Selassie, Babylon, Rasta! I've been waiting for my friends. Meet Joe and Slim. They'll also do it."

"Good, let me begin with you immediately."

The man ordered Bigboy to lie on a small bed in the corner whilst his friends looked on nervously.

"What's happening?" Slim's face was masked with worry.

"It's the new-do in town." The man whispered. "I'm going to tattoo him and pierce his ears."

Slim and Joe exploded into laughter. "But who said we like it?" Slim asked.

The man smeared the left ear lobe of Bigboy with a liquid and in a flash pierced the ear. Slim sizzled with fear; Joe's jaws hung loose with shock. Quickly the earring was fixed. The man gave a mirror to Bigboy who gazed at it and nodded with satisfaction. The man chuckled, "Yeah! Meerrh! Bigboy, you look handsome and smashing. The chicks will fight over you."

"I want the tattoo now." Bigboy put the mirror on the table.

"What type of design do you like and which part of your body?" the man gave a chart to Bigboy to study.

"Many like the bone-cross-bone and the pirate," The man pointed at them.

"The bone cross-bone will remind me of death," said Bigboy running his fingers on the chart until he settled on one. "Yes, I like the Scorpion. I want to sting."

"What do you want to sting?" Slim asked.

"I want to sting the chicks especially..."

Slim giggled foolishly. "I know the one you want to sting. I know the person you're doing this to attract. I know because of her you've pierced your ear and want to tattoo."

"It's Genevieve!" Joe whispered.

"Where do you want it?" The man was impatient.

"On his buttocks," Joe giggled.

"It'll be concealed," Slim said.

"I want it on my chest." Bigboy removed his shirt.

It took some time for the Scorpion to be tattooed on Bigboy and again when he looked into the mirror, he nodded with pleasure. "Yes, the next person." Bigboy ordered.

Slim cringed but Joe stepped forward. "I want to pierce my ear only. I don't need the tattoo now. BB, it'll cost you a lot."

"I'm paying for everything so take advantage."

"Ok! Then I'll need the eagle tattoo."

"Where?" the man squirted a smile.

"At my back."

"That's a useless place to have a tattoo. Nobody will see it. Have it on your chest too," Bigboy suggested.

"I suggest above the navel," Slim insisted.

"Yeah! It's a good place, Joe."

After it was done, Joe looked in the mirror and flashed rays of smiles. When Slim was invited, he shook his head, frowned, and bit his lips, "Don't know how my parents will take it."

"Why bring in parents?" Bigboy screamed. "It's the in-thing now and you're talking of parents who also had their time. You remember when I bought you your first jeans you said the same thing about parents not liking it, but they did in the end. We must set the agenda for our parents. My father told me in their time they wore bell-bottom trousers. C'mon, if you don't do it, you'll be odd among us."

"Then I'll have the tattoo only." Slim pleaded.

"No ways! You'll be odd and soon we would not like your company." Bigboy held Slim by the scruff of the neck. "You join us, or you leave. Why is it that we do things together and today you're refusing my clever idea? Look at how handsome Joe looks in his earring. Many chicks will adore him. Chicks will flock to you too. I'll pay for everything." Bigboy finally pushed Slim towards the bed.

Slim had a pirate tattooed at his back before his ear was pierced. The three boys looked at themselves in the mirror, smiled and patted themselves on their shoulders before they bade each other goodbye.

Slim was enveloped by the inky darkness of Sokora; he found it difficult to make his way home because there was a power outage in the neighbourhood. His home was equally dark, saved by a dwarfish candle struggling to emit its last light. Baba was indoors and his mother was lying on the sofa when Slim went to the kitchen to eat the usual *tuozafi* and the slippery vegetable soup. When he finished eating, he belched loudly and then felt some itches on his left earlobe which reminded him of the earring.

5

SKIRT AND BLOUSE

Abiba, the youngest sister of Slim, was the first person to see him that morning. Stunned, she stood for a long time and giggled. "Yakubu, you look like a woman now. Why did you leave the other ear? It's funny."

"Ssssh! Ssssh! You little parrot. Keep your mouth shut." Slim charged at Abiba who darted off screaming. "What's the problem?" Mma asked.

"Mma. Er---er---Yakubu is wearing earrings and he wants to beat me."

Mma dashed out, stole a quick glance at Slim, stood akimbo and was speechless. Her lips were quivering and her eyes bulging in their sockets. At last, she asked, "Is that my son Yakubu or Meri?"

There was silence as Slim took some steps backwards and leant against the door post. "Mma, why complain about this simple thing. It's the modern way of life."

"Modern my foot! Remove this ugly thing from your ear before your father sees it. Let me have the earring."

Slim shook his head. "What's all this, Mma? You people are too traditional and don't want to see change. Most of my friends' parents are not bothered by things like boys wearing earrings. You people must change with the times."

"Let me have the earring. After that you allow the sore to heal then the matter is ended. I'm waiting for you." Mma tried to remove the earring but Slim resisted.

Abiba was surprised when there was a little scuffle to collect the earring. She screamed, "Baaaba! Baaaba!"

Mma quickly dragged Slim into her room. "Look, if your father sees you, it will be thunder and lightning in this house. Just listen to me and take my orders. Remove the earring and let me hide it."

Baba banged the door and pushed it open, “What’s wrong?”

“It’s just a small issue I’m discussing with Yakubu.”

“What’s the issue?”

“Just leave the matter for me.”

“Are you hiding something from me?”

Mma quickly stood between Baba and Slim who was trying to remove the earring.

Angrily, Baba pushed Mma aside, saw the pierced ear and began to shake with rage. “What is this? Are you getting mad? Why do such a thing?” Baba lunged and held Slim by the neck. “Why this, tell me before I break your neck.”

Slim tried to struggle free, but the grip was so tight that it suffocated him. Finally, Baba loosened the grip a bit. “Tell me why you have pierced your ear!”

“It’s the latest fashion.”

“Nonsense! I’ll not tolerate this useless fashion under my roof.”

“Baba, many boys are doing it now. All the stars…”

“You don’t have to copy what other boys are doing. We’re not rich but we should have some standards to follow. Our culture and even our religion do not allow it. If boys start wearing earrings, how are we going to differentiate boys from girls? How can I differentiate you from Amina and Meri?

"Baba, boys pierce only one ear..."

Baba foamed with anger and squeezed Slim's neck and with the other hand tore the earring out. Slim squealed, struggled to set himself free from the painful grip and fled out of the house with his dripping, bloody ears.

Baba threw the earring into the coal pot. He washed his hands hurriedly, and the whole of that morning trembled with fear for his first son for whom he has sacrificed all the years from the primary school to the senior high school.

Slim had been an obedient, hard-working boy in school. The earring incident had made Baba to think deeply about the future of his son.

"Mma," Baba called. "You've been protecting this boy whenever he goes wrong. You're encouraging him to go astray. I don't want the younger ones to copy this bad behaviour afflicting the youth in the cities. What did you do when you saw your son wearing earring?"

"I advised him to remove the earring."

"Just advise?" Baba growled, "You should have hit his head with the nearest object."

"That would be too cruel. You know children of these modern times..."

"Stop defending bad behaviour! The world is turning upside down. If we're not careful, Yakubu will come home one day wearing skirt and blouse." Mma quaked with a giggle, "Don't think he'll go to such an extent."

"He has taken the first step. I'll not allow this under my roof. I'll keep an eagle eye on the children. We're not rich; our children are our wealth."

6

ONE FOR THE ROAD

Bigboy was the mother hen who always led the way and the two chicks, Slim and Joe followed. That afternoon, Bigboy was followed by only one chick, who was Joe. They tried several times to call Slim, but his phone was off. About an hour later, Slim called. "Where are you guys?"

"We're at Banana Beach Resort on the High Street. We're chilling, well, well, well."

"Will be there in a jiffy," Slim assured.

Bigboy smiled because he knew the best way to keep friends under his wings was to entice them with food and drinks. He had enjoyed the position where he was the only one who called the shots as the others looked on helplessly.

Whilst they waited for Slim, Bigboy ordered for two grilled guinea fowls then he clapped gently to draw the attention of the waiter. "What drinks do you have?"

The waiter pointed at the notice board on which the drinks were listed. Bigboy looked at it and smiled. "Charley, guys, today we have to raise the level a bit."

"I need a bottle of coke as usual," Joe said, "And what do you mean by raising the level?"

"I want to mix a little gin with Sprite to get the kick."

"You'll get drunk. Remember you said we're meeting Genevieve today."

"No problem at all. I want to be a little high."

"You get too high, you'll fall. Eh! Look at Slim coming."

No sooner had Slim sat down than Bigboy leered at Joe. "Look at Slim's torn ear without earrings. What happened? Tell us."

Slim narrated his encounter with his father as the two friends listened with rapt attention until Bigboy shouted, "I would have given my dad a blow on the face. Look, when I went home my dad liked my earring. He compared his earring to mine---"

"Has your dad pierced his ear?" Joe interrupted.

"Yes, my dad is up to date in all things. He has a gold ring in his ear. He promised getting me a gold earring soon. Slim, your father is too backward and needs to be brought to the twenty-first century. You told me your father is a bank manager so he should be aware of modern fashion and grooming. You see that Joe's mother is a modern woman, so Joe is still wearing his earring. Joe, what did your mother say?"

"When I got home, she looked at me coldly for a long time and just asked me to go for my supper."

Bigboy jumped and clapped, "Yeah! Yeah! She is a civilised woman. Slim, your father did not try at all. If I were you, I'll pierce the other ear to challenge him. We need our freedom from our parents."

The aroma of the grilled guinea fowl wafted in the air; Bigboy made sure the plate was placed in front of him. "I like the thighs of guinea fowls so they're for me." He picked one of the thighs, rubbed it in the pepper and onions and pulled the tough meat. He chewed hurriedly as his friends looked on eagerly, waiting for him to give the orders before they picked their portions. At last, he belched, then pointed at the plate before Slim and Joe picked their pieces.

Soon Bigboy finished the four thighs and went for another big piece. It was a race for the one who could chew quickly. Joe struggled with his meat which he had chewed for minutes. His jaws ached so he swallowed the meat forcibly and reached for another piece.

Slim smeared his piece with a lot of pepper and opened his mouth to draw in more air to cool his tongue. Despite the discomfort, he grabbed another chunk of meat and began to chew.

Bigboy called the waiter. “I want two tots of gin boxed with Sprite. Give my friends what they like.”

Joe sipped his Coke whilst Slim gulped his Fanta to cool his tongue which was raging with the heat from the pepper. Bigboy took a swig and frowned before he broke into a smile. “Oh! So nice and smooth and tickling on the tongue. Hmnn! I’ve not regretted the mixture.” Then Bigboy downed the rest of the drink and licked his tongue in excitement whilst Joe looked at him in admiration.

“Let’s have another round, waiter. This time give me four tots of gin and some Sprite. And give my friends a tot of gin and Coke. It's nice and smooth, Joe and Slim, try it."

"I'll mix my gin with Fanta," Joe nodded.

Slim was angry. "My religion forbids drinking; I'll settle for Coke this time."

"OK. You always want to be different and remain backward. Waiter, give him a crate of Coke."

Joe's eyes shone with excitement in their sockets. "The mixture is perfect and it's warming my body. Oh! It's so smooth! I feel like dancing to some good music."

"DJ! Give us some good music." Bigboy screamed.

Soon, loud music blared from the speakers nearby. Joe listened and began to tap his feet. Suddenly, he jumped to his feet and began to dance.

Bigboy snapped his thumb and forefinger, and then also jumped to his feet to join Joe. Gripped by the atmosphere, Slim also heaved his waist, clapped then joined them. They danced for a long time until Bigboy began to sweat and breathe furiously. "Waiter! come and fuel us. I need four tots. Yaaah! Yaaah! Yaaaaah! I need it raw this time to get the kick. And Joe what do you need…er… place your order."

"I need four tots and ice-cubes. Yeaaah! Mennnn! Sheeet!" Joe screamed and spat.

"Yeah! Mennnn! Brother Mennn! We're really chilling. Oh! What a lovely day. I can feel the breeze from the sea. I feel like swimming." Bigboy screamed at the open sea. "I feel like a man now. I'm confident now..."

"Afraid boy! I know why you're charging your body." Slim teased.

Bigboy laughed loudly and took a deep gulp of the drink; he beat his chest in excitement. "Yes, today is the day of all days. I must win today...er...dee jay let the music flow. Give us some rap music."

When they began to dance again Bigboy waved the waiter, "Come and give us one for the road."

"You're drinking too much," Slim whispered.

"Shut up, Slim. Is it your money? Is it your body? Shame on you, always backsliding..."

"Bigboy, you must listen to me. From here we're going on a very important mission. Let's get going soon." Slim got up and headed towards the washroom.

The waiter was ready with the bottle of gin. Bigboy took four tots and Joe ordered two tots. Then Bigboy drew nearer to the waiter and whispered, "Pour four tots quickly into that Coke." The waiter obeyed.

When Slim returned, he picked his drink and gulped it quickly; he frowned and then hissed. “Hmnn! The coke is flat and bitter now. We’ve been here for some time now. We must go.”

Bigboy burst into laughter, clapped, and spat. “I’m a man now. I feel like jumping into the sea and swim and swim and swim all over the world.”

As they made their way out, Slim staggered, sat back in his chair and placed his head on the table. Bigboy and Joe stopped, rushed to the scene, and rammed Slim on the shoulders. “Get up Slim! You did not taste any alcohol, yet you’re drunk.”

“I’m feeling dizzy; my face is turning round and round. The sea is red, and the trees are jumping.” Slim cried.

Bigboy and Joe dragged Slim who tottered behind them to the High Street where they hired a taxi to continue their rounds.

7

TRUTH

Genevieve, browsing through a magazine, was already seated in the restaurant. Immediately Bigboy set his eyes on her from afar, excitement gripped him, and he rubbed his palms vigorously. "Sssshh! Yeah! She's in. She's in the net. Today is the day. I've got her today. Yeah! Yeah! I am going to get her today and kiss her and hug her and---"

"Ssssh! BB, stop that. You're talking too loud for her to hear. Don't cheapen yourself at all. You must be bold and courteous today. I trust you, BB. No fears at all.

Give her sweet words to win her. Girls love to be praised so heap praises on her. She'll like the earring and don't forget to expose the tattoo on your chest to show that you're abreast with time."

Obediently, Bigboy unbuttoned his shirt and wiped the sweat off his chest. Slim staggered into the restaurant, sat at a corner and placed his head on the table. Strangely, Bigboy was confused and just stood still, and stared at Genevieve when he got closer. Sweat poured freely from his face, and he sneezed uncontrollably. Joe was angry and nudged Bigboy in the ribs. "Are you afraid, BB? Why are you standing like a policeman on duty? C'mon move. We're behind you so don't disgrace us. Move like a gentleman to her now. You're sweating too much, wipe your face and put a smile on your sour face."

Bigboy wiped his face briskly and sneezed whilst Joe tiptoed after him. "Your handkerchief is too dirty, hide it. There is the guinea fowl pepper in it. Take mine."

Shivering, Bigboy staggered towards Genevieve whilst Joe kept whispering to him to be bold and gentle. At last, Bigboy's legs quivered to a halt. "Hello Genevieve! Sweetie! wonderful to meet you. You're super gorgeous in the most beautiful red blouse I've ever seen. You are my rose and er—er-- look sweet and you look splendid like an angel from heaven." He seized her hand and squeezed it. "Oh! Your palms are as soft as cotton wool and your smiles are like sunshine in my heart..."

Genevieve frowned. "Enough of your praise! BB. Naive girls like these praises. You don't keep to time at all. We agreed to meet at three o'clock."

"I thought it was four," Bigboy unfastened another button on his shirt to expose his shiny, bloated, tummy but Genevieve pretended not to look at it. She looked at Bigboy eyeball to eyeball and giggled. "BB, when did you piercc your ear?" Proudly, Bigboy held the lobe of his ear. "Er---recently"

"Why do this?"

"Er---you know, it's the in-thing now."

"Are you sure you are not copying blindly?"

"No! All the best-selling musicians and top soccer stars are wearing earrings..."

"It doesn't appeal to me. If you go with me home and my parents see this, they will order you out."

"Your parents don't like it. Do you like it?"

"I hate it more than my parents. BB, do your parents like it?"

"Yeah! My dad likes it. He also wears earrings."

Genevieve was appalled. "Hmnn! What sort of family do you come from? And did they look on for you to do these things on your body? I'm even scared of the nasty tattoo on your chest. Armed robbers tattoo their bodies. Aren't you copying blindly?"

Bigboy was dumb and confused. Ashamed, he turned to look at Joe, who was eavesdropping, and who had secretly removed his earring and buttoned his shirt tightly. Bigboy felt betrayed when he realised, he was the only one wearing earring. At once he felt lonely and stared at Genevieve in confusion and muttered, "I thought it was the current fashion."

Genevieve was getting impatient as she looked at Bigboy sternly. "I'm disappointed today, BB. I've always respected you and thought you come from a responsible home but look at what you've shown me today. You have pierced your ear, tattooed and the most irresponsible act of all is that you're drunk."

"I swear! I'm not drunk..."

"You smell of alcohol. The moment you entered the room I smelt it. The drink is following you like a smoke. And it's a pity that the two of you are drunk."

"I took only soft drinks," Joe grinned.

"You're also full of alcohol except the one who is sleeping over there. You two are all drunk. It's shameful."

"I'm telling you we took soft drinks," Bigboy said brusquely.

"I hate liars. I trust people who admit their fault. Your denial is making me angry."

"We took only two tots of gin," Joe mumbled.

"Shut up! You took it alone. I'm a clean guy."

"Gentlemen, I think I must go home now. It's getting late and my parents are strict about my outings. Goodbye till we meet again. Take care of yourselves so that you're not knocked down by a vehicle."

Dejected, Bigboy was trapped in the chair for a long time, then looked at Joe angrily. "You've betrayed me. Why admit that we drank some gin? You've spoilt my chances today."

"BB don't blame me. You asked for the gin first. Then you forced me to take some of the gin."

"Why do you have to admit in front of a girl I am in love with? Why didn't you keep your mouth shut and you rush in to admit that we drank alcohol?"

"There are moments you must speak the truth if you're found out. I did that. My mother always tells me to speak the truth. I always tell the truth. Truth must be told and that was what I did to save the situation."

"You did not save any situation! You blocked my chances and made my Genevieve angry. I've been planning for Genevieve all these months and today is the day to seal the deal, then you come and damage things."

"BB, I've not wronged you. You said you wanted to fortify yourself to meet Genevieve and you went beyond limits."

"You've wronged me also on the issue of the earrings. Why did you remove yours to make me look like the only culprit? Why didn't you leave it in your ears? Are you telling me you're not wearing it again?"

"I don't think I'll wear the earring again."

"Why are you changing because Genevieve did not like earrings?"

"My family and community hate it. Some girls have been jeering at me. Some of my mother's friends have called me and admonished me. I feel very uncomfortable in the earrings..."

Bigboy got up, walked towards Slim, who was still sleeping and dragged him. "Hey! You get up. It's time to go."

8

THE VIGIL

Slim wobbled on his feet when he got out of the taxi at Sokora bus stop. Bigboy and Joe held him to stand upright but he slumped and crashed to the ground. Bigboy fumed. “Hey! Slim, don’t waste our time. Where is the direction to your house?”

“My house is there.” Slim pointed at the inky darkness.

“Which street’? What’s the house number?”

Slim spat out big phlegm. “We don’t have street names.”

“House number?” Joe interjected.

"Our houses are not numbered."

Bigboy was angry. "What a place! It is crowded, dark and dangerous."

"It's too noisy for my liking." Joe said.

Slim coughed suddenly and clutched his stomach. "I feel like vomiting…" He wriggled himself free from the grip of Bigboy, crouched on the ground and vomited into a choked, steamy gutter.

Bigboy was getting apprehensive, so he gripped Slim and jerked him to his feet. "Don't waste our time. C'mon, lead us to your house."

Slim led them through the dark, muddy, alley until they reached the mosque where the muezzin was calling the faithful for prayers. Slim hesitated and turned sharply into a smaller alley opposite the mosque. "Don't want my people to see me drunk. The Imam is my father's friend."

"Who said you're drunk? You're feeling dizzy," said Bigboy. "I'm getting scared of this place. We can't go further. Slim, I think you can find your way home. It's your territory. Bye, Slim."

Panting for breath, Bigboy led Joe as they groped their way back towards the busy street. Bigboy oozed sweat in torrents from his face and his handkerchief could not stem the tide. "Joe, I'm surprised where Slim lives. He's always throwing his weight around that he lives in a big flat in Sokora. The houses I've seen so far are too tiny and unplanned."

Joe smirked. "You know when we're in a group and especially when the chicks are around, Slim must boast to be somebody. You remember when we met Genevieve some time ago at the musical night at TV 4 studio; Slim boasted that his father was a rich bank manager. That day the girls believed Slim and nearly fell in love with him."

"I think it's better to be true to oneself and let people know who we are than faking things all around us. Slim has surprised me. Is it good to trust people like that?"

Bigboy smiled. "There are some people who want to put on airs around them. It's their own headache. I hate people who claim to be what they're not. It's not a good thing at all. I'm plain and frank about things. I dislike the cover up."

They did not talk again when they were in the taxi towards the central business district. Bigboy patted Joe on the back when they got down. "Bye Joe. Let's meet tomorrow at the new KFC joint. They've just opened and running some specials."

"What's this KFC?"

"You're out of the city. Haven't you heard the advert on all the FM stations? It's the latest chicken joint in the city."

"I see but what's the meaning of the KFC?"

"You'll pay me for teaching you. Are you ready to pay?"

"Teach me and I pay later."

Bigboy whispered, "It means Kentucky Fried Chicken. We meet there tomorrow at ten sharp." Joe gave the thumps up and left.

Back in Sokora, Slim staggered in the alley, stepped into a muddy pool of water, and crashed to the ground. He lay in the mud and tried to get back on his feet but despite all the attempts he made, he slipped back. Slim gave up and coiled in the mud until he felt a hand tapping him. The strange hands jerked him up and held him upright. "Who're you? Why are you blocking our path? Where are you going?"

"I'm Yakubu. Please direct me to my house."

"Where is your house?"

"It's near the big gutter and the school."

"You're lost. You must go back; turn left, then right, then go ahead and turn right before left again..."

"I'm confused. Please help me..."

"You're drunk, young man..."

"I'm not drunk. It's only my face which is turning round and round..."

"So, your face decided to turn? Stop it from turning round. You smell of alcohol yet you're denying you're drunk."

"I swear I'm not drunk. I'm just feeling dizzy and feel like throwing up..."

"Shut up! You must accept you're drunk and need some help. This is a bad way to lead your life as a young person."

"I'll not shut up! I'm not drunk. I can see you're turning round and round. You're drunk. Leave me alone."

The man released his support and Slim crashed into the mud again. He slept for some time until he felt the mosquito bites and woke up. The weakness and the nauseating feeling had eased, and Slim could see his surroundings clearly. He could not guess the time because it was quiet, cold, and hazy around him. He remembered his mobile phone and looked for it frantically, but his pockets were empty. His heart started to beat fast, and he began to sweat suddenly.

Gradually, Slim was back on his feet and wound his way towards the house. His head was reeling with the images of the day. He could recall the beach, then the guinea fowl and then the music. Then he recalled Genevieve in the restaurant, then his mind went blank.

As he neared his house, he began to think of his parents. Slim opened his eyes widely to test that he was not dreaming. He could see his house and the flicker of light through an opening on the main door. He stood by the door, his hands shivering when he tried to knock. Slim was stricken with fear and his legs began to melt once more. The dizziness and the nauseating feeling which churned in his stomach began again. Slim leant against the door, knocked gently then the door creaked. Once he stepped in, he crashed onto the floor. He lay there quivering and suddenly he gushed out the last remnants of the guinea fowl he had eaten in the afternoon.

Mma was shaken with fear. Her feet were sinking under her because her only son had come home drunk and dirty that dawn. Mma had to think fast what to do. At first, she dragged her son gently to his room but realised it was not safe because in the next room was Baba who was snoring loudly. He had waited for his son for such a long time and charged with anger, locked the main door. Baba had warned Mma nobody should open the door for Yakubu.

At last, Mma thought of the best way to protect her son; she led him to sleep on a mat in her room. As Mma kept vigil, she saw a strange thing which terrified her. The tattoo on Yakubu's back! Quickly she covered the tattoo with the shirt.

9

FORGIVE ME

Mma looked at the time; it was an hour before the first dawn prayer. She had to be quick before her husband Baba went to the mosque nearby. Baba had been a devout Muslim all his life and the community admired him to such an extent that on many occasions when the Imam was absent Baba led the faithful in prayers.

Mma made sure Slim had a quick bath and changed his clothes. Then she prepared some tea which revived Slim back to life. Mma looked at her son accusingly.

"My son, I saw a devilish mark at your back. You must make sure your father does not see it. Now what do we tell your father about your arrival late to the house? He'll be ready for prayers soon. If he hears you've tasted alcohol the house will be in flames, and he can disown you. It will also be an embarrassment to him as one of the Muslims respected in the society."

"I'll tell Baba I went somewhere with my friends and the traffic was heavy and as a result..."

"Be serious, Yakubu. Think of something to hide the suspicion else we'll be sent running for cover in this house."

Slim was silent for some time; he could not come out with a good excuse. At last, he said, "What if I tell him I was ill and was hospitalised for some time."

"That will not convince your father. He is a meticulous person and will go to the extent of looking for the hospital you were admitted, the prescription given to you and even the doctor who treated you."

Slim had run out of ideas; he looked at his mother helplessly. "Mma, please help me as you've been doing on many occasions. You always come with better excuses to convince Baba."

Mma thought for a while; she looked at the time ticking away then whispered, "I have an idea. Let's tell him you were attacked by thieves on your way home. The cuts on your face and the small swellings on your hands will convince him. When he questions you, don't talk to him directly else, he'll pick the scent."

"Mma, you always save me from trouble. It's the best excuse…"

"Hurry up. Go and brush your teeth to stop the smell of alcohol."

Slim rushed out of his mother's room when he heard the key clicking in his father's door. He missed his father by a hair's breadth. He could hear the father's footsteps towards Mma's room.

"Has the devil returned?" he asked Mma.

"Yes, he…"

"How did he enter the house? Who opened the door for him? I gave clear instructions that he should be locked out. Did you open the door for him?"

Mma was speechless, confused and wrung her hands in despair. Baba was furious and walked briskly towards Mma. "I'm asking you a simple question. Did you open the door for Yakubu?"

Mma's voice quivered; her legs began sinking into the floor. "He kept knocking and knocking so I had to open."

"You've been a very stubborn woman, always shielding Yakubu. You did the same thing when he wore earrings. Are you now the head of the house?"

Mma's face drooled with tears when she realized Slim would be led into a trap if she did not play her protective role well. Mma recalled the many years she had lived with Baba, a very strict man, who believed the family should be raised in the Muslim faith. He always made sure that the family said their prayers.

Mma had been a housewife who looked after the needs of the family. But there was a strange behaviour Baba showed anytime he was angry. He would glare at Mma, chew his lower lips, frown, and bite a piece of kola nut hurriedly. "Call Yakubu for me!"

Mma dashed to the door and called her son who appeared with dreary eyes. Baba looked at Slim from head to toe. "Your days are numbered in this house if you don't want to take instructions from me. Where did you go yesterday? I want you as a devout Muslim to speak the truth before Allah. Curse be unto you if you tell lies..."

"Baba don't curse your son," Mma interrupted.

"Shut up! A word from you again and I'll show you the way out. I'm getting tired of you these days..."

"I know you're tired of me. When you married me at the tender age you have forgotten the golden years. Have you not married your fourth wife who is younger?"

"I have the right to marry, and you don't have a say. I'll go ahead and marry more. I don't need your permission."

"Go ahead and marry hundred women. Do you have the money to support these children?"

"Are you starving in this house? For the past eighteen years I've fed, clothed, and done all that you need. I've sent my children to school and paid their fees from the little I earn. I don't go about begging. I'm a responsible man in this community. I'm not like my elder brother who has abandoned his children."

Slim was quiet like a mouse enjoying the duel; he prayed that the quarrel should become more heated so that he would no longer be the focus of his father's answer. But suddenly, his father fixed his gaze on him for a long time. Slim could not look his father in the face; he cast his gaze on the floor and saw a cockroach scuttling on the linoleum carpet. Slim raised his leg high and crushed the insect into a pulp.

Baba was startled by the noise. "What do you think you're doing?"

"It's a cockroach, Baba."

"I asked you a question and I'm waiting for an answer now."

Slim was bewildered and his head began to spin on his body whilst Baba was waiting impatiently for an answer. "Can't you tell me where you went yesterday?"

Slim could hear the voice of Allah ringing in his head to speak the truth as a devout Muslim so that he would be free. The truth meant telling Baba he drank alcohol which was forbidden by his faith. It meant Baba could take a very drastic action against him. Slim heard another voice which drowned the voice of Allah urging him to hide the truth and be free. Caught up in this quandary, Slim turned to look at Mma for the last time. Mma winked and frowned suddenly that early morning. Between the glare of Baba and the sinister look of Mma, Slim crumbled and gasped for breath. He mumbled and tears snaked on his face. "I did not hear you at all," Baba bellowed, "Just speak the truth clearly and loudly before your God."

Mma coughed harshly and cast her last dark gaze which made Slim to tremble. Suddenly he said boldly, "Baba, I was attacked on my way home and lay unconscious for hours."

"Are you sure you're speaking the truth before you and your God?"

"Yes, Baba." At once, Slim felt a tremor under his feet which made him feel like sinking into the ground. When he looked through the window, he saw truth like a bird flying out.

Baba glared at Slim for the last time, turned and walked towards the mosque. Slim looked at Mma and suddenly felt guilt filling his body to the brim. The guilt weighed him down and for a while Slim could not take a step. When he tried to move, his leg was like lead. The tears flowed in torrents on his face as he made the first steps to leave the house to join his father in the mosque.

Slim made the ablutions and entered the mosque. He raised his hands in prayers, knelt, and tried to pray. What should he tell God when some minutes before he had not been truthful? Should he take advantage now and confess to his God? Slim panicked when he saw his father close to him. The guilt began to flood him again, so he turned his gaze at the Imam leading the prayers.

Suddenly prayer popped in his head then he clasped his hands on his chest and whispered, "Allah, forgive me for the lies I told this morning. I could not help it. It is better to tell you the truth directly than through my father. Allah, forgive me." A sudden exhilaration rushed through his body; he felt the guilt in his body being mopped away. Slim floated like a feather when he skipped out of the mosque.

10

EXCUSES

Genevieve was down with malaria since that meeting with Bigboy at the restaurant. She had called Esi, her bosom friend, with whom she shared secrets, several times but no response. Esi had deposited all her secret encounters into the ears of Genevieve for safe keeping. The hottest secret Esi had deposited recently was about a boy who had cried in front of her and offered her money just to fall in love with him. Genevieve was eager to meet Esi after a long silence so when her phone rang that morning, she was all smiles. “Esi! I can’t believe you’ve neglected me all this while.”

“Was busy. I’m on my way to your house now. I have the latest and the hottest news for you, Gene.”

“Please hurry up. I’m itching.’

Genevieve was always excited anytime Esi paid a visit. Quickly she cleaned the old, torn sofa and carried it under the coconut tree on their compound. She was all ears, waiting for Esi to arrive so when the gate rattled, Genevieve rushed to give her a hug. “My long, lost buddy. Esi, you’re welcome. And am seeing the new hairstyle. Hmnn! Lovely weave on. Indian or Dubai?”

“Give me some water to drink before I tell you about the hair.”

Esi gulped the water and heaved a sigh. “Gene, this hair is Brazilian human hair.” She was emphatic. Genevieve ran her fingers through the strands as Esi turned her head gently from side to side. A streak of jealousy flowed on Genevieve’s face when she finally left the last strand. “It must be expensive, Esi.”

“Very expensive and the new craze in the city now.”

Genevieve knew how to prod the conversation, so she nudged Esi gently in the ribs and whispered, “I know somebody sponsored this hair.”

"You're right. There is this crazy guy working in one of the banks in the city. I can't even remember the name of the bank. He is jumping all over me and you know me as usual, I know how to shrug him off."

"I trust you for that. But you must have a crush for one of these men knocking at your door. You must settle on one."

"Hmnn! Still searching for Mr. Right. The day is still young, we have many years to make a choice."

"What is the latest hot news you want to tell me? I'm eager." Genevieve stoked the conversation.

"I'm more eager than you. You must tell me in detail how the meeting with Bigboy, our loud-mouthed classmate went."

"Are you eager for dead news? It was a disaster."

"Just give me the detail."

Genevieve was caught in a trap, so she began the narrative in a jerky way until she got to the point where she had to lower her voice. "And BB was drunk, had a tattoo and wore earrings."

Esi erupted into laughter, tears welling in her eyes. "I personally don't mind the tattoo. I admire it…"

"What about a boy wearing earrings?" Genevieve interrupted.

"I don't care about earrings too. As for alcohol I can't stand it. So, what did you do to Bigboy, the guy who likes to sponsor you in school? Who showers you with gifts you don't turn down? I remember the ice-creams and the pizzas he arranged for you some of the weekends..."

"Stop that. We ate the goodies together."

"Just want to know what you did when you realised, he had taken alcohol."

"I really gave it to him and left the restaurant. He was with Slim and another guy. Slim was so shy that he put his head on the table pretending to be asleep."

"Who is Slim?"

"Have you forgotten Yakubu, the brilliant boy in our class? His nickname is Slim because he is thin like a blade of grass."

Esi giggled. "I used to wonder why a hungry-looking boy should be topping the class in some subjects. Have you contacted Bigboy since?"

"No! I am disappointed in him."

"I've told you many times that our classmates are not our serious partners and that we should deal with adults who are working and can sponsor us. These boys cannot even buy lunch. You know Kwaku, our mate, promised me a wonderful gift. I was on cloud nine. Guess what he gave me before he made a proposal."

"Did he buy you a take-away lunch pack?"

"You've gone too high." Esi giggled.

"Why are you laughing? Was it a funny gift?"

"Very funny and insulting."

"Just tell me."

"Chewing gum."

They burst into laughter, Esi dabbing her tears with a handkerchief. "That is what the boy can afford. It's truly from his heart. Did you accept it?"

"I collected it from him, dropped it on the ground and stepped on it."

"Oh! Why do that to hurt the poor boy's feelings?"

"Gene, we want the wonderful things in life and these boys keep harassing us with pens, handkerchiefs, and chocolates. I've grown past these. I need lavish things to enjoy life."

Genevieve stared at her friend and was astonished. "I would have accepted it as long as I know it is from the person's heart."

"You have low standards. I've tried to fix you all this time but you're still very difficult. The one which hurt me most was the businessman you turned down last time. You'll have been swimming in money by now. The man used to give me gifts but because you turned him down, he has ceased to do so."

"I'm scared because I can land in trouble."

"You're always afraid of pregnancy but there are now tablets to sort it out."

Genevieve's eyes opened widely, and she began to sweat. She stood akimbo and paced up and down. "Gene, that is what I fear most. You're my bosom friend and you're the only person who knows about my family background."

Esi's eyes flooded with tears; she also got up from the sofa, held Genevieve's hand gently and ushered her back to sit down. "I know you're my one and only friend and will not hurt you in any way. By the way since you want to be with the boys, is that the end of your relationship with Bigboy? You can still give him a try. If I, were you, I would give him stiff conditions and recommend that he stops drinking."

"Esi, I am disappointed. My mind is no longer about relationships…"

"Don't be disappointed," Esi interrupted, "Bigboy is in your heart. If he is not, then I still suggest you try the adults…"

"Esi, enough of BB. Let's talk about something else."

Just then there was a purr from Esi's bag. She quickly picked the mobile phone, read the text message, and said, "This crazy old man who is of the same age as my grandfather is bombarding me with text messages…"

"Hmnnn! A new catch?"

"I can't catch an old grandfather. He is loaded with cash and doesn't know what to do with it. He bought this latest iPhone for me."

"Eheh! Where did you meet him?"

"At a wedding reception and he has been harassing me since, but I know how to juggle them so that they're always in suspense. I'm careful not to give myself to them."

"How do you go about it?"

"Excuses, excuses, more excuses…"

"Such as?"

"There are tons of them. I have period pains; malaria, travelling and of late I put them off that I'm recovering from typhoid."

Genevieve laughed heartily. She could imagine Esi running from one partner to the next, whispering excuses into their ears and the men nodding with pleasure. At once Genevieve picked the mobile phone and scrutinised it carefully. The pangs of jealousy hit Genevieve once more. She was speechless as she looked at the sophisticated icons on the phone. "Esi, you're affable and a nice-looking girl, that is why the men flock to you. I'm a girl but I admire your facial looks, the dimple on your right cheek and your height. Even the way you walk is full of confidence..."

"Don't belittle yourself, Gene. Every human being is beautiful. You also have some qualities I admire about you. Do you know that I like your bright, clear eyes and your sleek fingers and your shapely legs?"

Genevieve puffed with pride and smiled. She looked at her fingers carefully and said, "BB is crazy about my fingers. Anytime I meet him, he always wants to touch my fingers."

The phone rang but Esi did not pick the call. The incessant call continued until it stopped. "The grandfather is the one calling. He puts me off."

"But he gives you beautiful things..."

"I did not request for them."

The ringtone tore the air again. Esi picked the call and again it was from the old man. Her fingers froze and there was lump in her throat. For minutes the old man ranted whilst Esi listened attentively. Then she said, “Yes, I have appointment to meet you at the motel this afternoon, but my best friend called Genevieve is admitted at the hospital and I am with her now. Can we make another appointment tomorrow?”

Esi tittered when the call was over. Then she looked at her time. “I must go now. Gene, tomorrow you’ll go with me on a special mission.”

11

GREENHORN

Joe met Bigboy at a nearby Internet café. It was a steamy room, and a dangling fan squeaked and churned the air. Joe booted the computer; the bluish screen blinked several times until it became clear. Clicking the mouse, Joe selected the website and got to his E-mail inbox. He clicked on the name and the message was clear.

My sweetheart Lucy, I am planning to send you the amount of $4,000 by express MoneyGram. You should receive it by Thursday to pay for your hospital bill. I was very sad to learn you were admitted and will do everything to help you and make you happy. I am arranging for your air ticket so that you come to visit me during the summer. With much love. Smith

Joe's face brightened with smiles as he read the message a second and third time. He rubbed his palms together and whispered to Bigboy. "Good news, my good friend BB. By tomorrow I'll be smiling all the way to the bank. We're really going to chill and chill and chill and party and party. I'll spoil you tomorrow. Read the message."

Bigboy read the message and was perplexed. "Hmnn! Why is he calling you Lucy instead of Joe? Are you sure you're the one?"

"Sshhh! I'm the one. Charley, let's go out and I will brief you."

Bigboy was anxious but Joe kept him at bay and continued eating his pie at the restaurant. When he had had enough of the pie and gulped the guava juice drink, he smacked his lips. "I'm surprised you've not heard of the latest Internet deal which is all over these days."

"I've heard of Sakawa…"

"What I'm doing is not Sakawa. With Sakawa you must go the occult way to sleep in the cemetery, make love to mad women and obtain body parts for rituals. Mine is using the brains to swindle people."

Joe told Bigboy he used the picture of his younger sister Sally to lure Smith who thought he was communicating with a girl. Smith had fallen in love with the created person Lucy and was eager to go into a deep relationship ending in marriage. As the relationship deepened Smith had requested Lucy to send a nude picture to him.

"Did you send it?"

"Yes, I did..."

"That's bad, Joe. Why subject your sister to this humiliation for money?"

Joe giggled. "BB, you're still green in this new deal. Greenhorn, are you worried?"

"But you did send the nude picture to..."

"Take it easy," Joe interrupted, "There is a way of going about it."

"Tell me. I'm still suspicious."

"We do what is known in IT as photoshop. I picked a nude picture from a magazine, edited it by transferring my sister's face onto it. Did some graphic colouring to match the skin colour and it was perfect. Smith was so excited that he told me the picture was always at his bedside."

"You're smart in this. You're really using your brains. Do many people know about this?"

"Not too many boys are in it yet. I'm one of the early birds. The deal is now spreading. Do you want me to introduce you to it?"

"I'm not interested. My dad provides the money I need."

"But you need your own money to spend freely."

"Do you think I can make enough money?"

"Lots of money. Last week one boy living near my house swindled somebody overseas for half a million dollars."

"Are you serious?"

"Very serious. The boy sent messages round that a huge sum of money in a Swiss bank belonging to a dead African head of state has been transferred into his account. To withdraw the money, he needed some people abroad to show their account number and the money transferred into the account and shared. When thousands of dollars poured to help the withdrawal, he closed the contact. The boy has bought the latest sports car. He has stopped school and always playing music and roaming in town in the sports car. He told me he has eighteen girlfriends."

"He's crazy to stop school. He should have enrolled in the most expensive school. Are you also aiming at one million dollars?"

"Of course. You begin with small requests such as hospital bills then you wait and see if the person will respond. Once he sends the money, you wait for some time and then put in another request."

"Are you going to put in another request?"

"I have the second request ready."

"What's it?"

"I'll let him send thc air ticket for my visit. Then I'll book the flight but will not board the plane. I'll wait for some days to make him anxious then will take a picture of a crashed car and send it to him."

Bigboy shook his head and smiled. "What do you mean by this?"

Joe tapped Bigboy on the shoulder and said, "It means on my way to the airport I had a terrible accident but was saved by the airbag. He'll then send money for my hospital expenses and then pay for a new car."

"Eeh! You're crafty. Be careful."

"Don't worry at all. When I've extracted enough money from him, I'll close the E-mail contact, then the whole relationship ends."

They left the fast-food joint on their way to the shopping mall. Bigboy said he had seen a designer wristwatch from Switzerland which he would like to buy.

Slim had been unable to link up with his friends by phone since the alcohol episode. Suddenly, Slim had become aloof and very bitter. For many days he recollected what might have happened on that day. The whole experience puzzled him because he did not understand that ordinary coke or Fanta, he always drank could knock him down.

Slim knew the places they usually visited on some days. Since it was a Wednesday, he knew that Bigboy usually gambled at the Afrique Pub. Slim remembered vividly Bigboy once devoured twelve sticks of beef *kebab* at that Pub.

Slim's guess was right when he reached the spot. Bigboy cracked a teasing laugh when he saw Slim. "Hey Slim! Very long time! Welcome! Shame, the man who could not trace his house! Meet the man who vomited and collapsed on the way. You're welcome, Slim. Long-time."

Slim frowned. "BB, no time for jokes. I'm here to ask you a question. Did you lace my drink with alcohol?" Joe froze with fear and winked secretly at Slim whilst Bigboy's face turned pale. "Be serious, Slim. I swear I didn't do that. You can ask Joe who was a witness."

Joe was edgy; his lips twitched rapidly then he scowled at Slim. "Er—er---I'm---er---you know we got drunk that day and---er---that's all that I can say."

"BB, you're a treacherous guy. Do you see how confused you look? How dare you do that to me when you know my religion forbids it?"

"Hey Slim! Do you know the person you're talking to? How dare you talk to me like that? Remember I've been supporting you all this time. I've opened your eyes and today you have the guts to confront me. Who are you at all? You dirty boy from the slums. Look at the jeans you're wearing and stop talking to me like that. I made you eat your first ice-cream and yoghurt and---"

"I'll not shut up, BB. You're a dangerous person. You're not reliable. I'll part ways with you today. To hell with your jeans and ice-creams."

Bigboy lunged at Slim and slapped him on the face. "You poor, dirty boy!"

Though Slim was dazed, he quickly jumped and kicked Bigboy in the face. Bigboy screamed and crashed to the ground. Joe quickly held Slim and mumbled, "It was BB's idea."

Slim freed himself from the grips of Joe, looked at Bigboy who was still moaning and rolling on the ground. "I'll not be in your company again." Slim walked away triumphantly.

12
OCTOPUS

They met at exactly ten o'clock at the Body talk boutique where Esi bought some designer jeans, perfumes and "T" shirt which had just arrived from London and Paris. Esi counted the crisp notes and gave it to the owner of the boutique. "Next week, when the new consignment of goods arrive, I'll give you a shout."

"I can give you the deposit for the Christian Dior sunshade and the Da Viva ostrich-skin handbag." Esi opened her purse stuffed with notes.

"I don't need a deposit from a regular customer like you. Once the goods arrive, I'll reserve them for you."

Esi stopped a taxi and told the driver to take the Beach Road. The driver was nervous and asked where they were going. "Just drive ahead. I'll tell you to stop when we get to the place."

The driver nodded and did not ask any question again until when they reached The Crystal Pleasure Beach, Esi ordered him to stop. Esi skipped ahead whilst Genevieve followed obediently.

They ordered some lemon drinks and pie. Esi was very apprehensive making calls and texting messages. Genevieve looked round the restaurant and was pleased with her new surroundings- the romantic music, dim lights and the waiters in their white, crisp uniforms who were very friendly and polite. Genevieve enjoyed the pie and wished for a second one.

No sooner had Esi finished her last call than a bald elderly white man limped in. Quickly, Esi got up, hugged, kissed him on the cheek and patted him lovingly on the back. The white man grinned with pleasure exposing his long, metallic, yellowish teeth.

"Jim, you're welcome to our country. We've been linking on the net all these months. Feel at home."

"I feel at home. The weather is humid, and I've never sweated like this before. The country is like a huge sauna bath, but the people are friendly. I'll get tanned nicely here."

When it was time to order for lunch, Genevieve ordered for plain rice and chicken. Esi nudged her and called her aside. "Order for something expensive. This is not the day to eat rice which is something we eat every day."

"What should I order?" Genevieve was nervous.

"Eat something like grilled octopus, oysters, prawns, smoked salmon and vegetables à la carte."

"I've never eaten these before."

"Try it. You're always scared of trying new things. This man is prepared to spend, so eat delicious things."

"Alright, I'll do so."

Surprisingly, Genevieve enjoyed the exotic food and wished she had that for meals daily. Jim was equally excited and was finding it difficult to know who Esi or Genevieve was. But for a long time, throughout the chat, Jim's gaze was fixed on Genevieve until he got up briefly to make his bookings for a room in the hotel.

"Esi, this man should be over eighty years old. I feel pity for him. Look at his pale face and his pink pointed nose…"

"Ssshhh! Don't mind the age, mind the money." Esi smirked as she looked at the old, white man drenched in sweat.

"This one is our great-grandfather."

"Do you know he emailed me that we should marry? He has come down for the wedding."

"Eh! People would throw stones at you. Are you prepared to marry him?"

"I'll marry his money."

The whole relationship between Esi and Jim started when Esi was facing financial problems at home. She killed her boredom by browsing on the net, then came across the request on Facebook. Quickly, Esi exchanged her contact with Jim, and they had been communicating for many months until Jim expressed the desire to visit her.

Jim had entered the spider's web and Esi, like the spider had begun to wrap the yarn around him until such time that she would strike Jim with the venom to paralyse him into coma to spend all his resources on her.

13
MALARIA

Joe cashed the money early that morning at a foreign exchange bureau. He pushed the bulged wallet into his back pocket and touched it often because he had not carried such a huge amount of money in his life. As he picked his way through the crowd at the busy market square, he avoided brushing himself against pedestrians. Suddenly he had developed suspicion for any person who got closer to him. He was careful about a young man hawking handkerchiefs who was following him for a long time. Joe stopped abruptly. "Why are you following me all this time?" The hawker did not mind at all, he hurriedly passed by and dissolved into the teeming crowd.

When Joe reached the High Street, he stopped a taxi. "I want to charter you the full day to transact my business. First take me to the Pleasure Beach Hotel. I want to take my breakfast there."

Joe was at the back seat feeling very pompous and barking instructions. "Hey! Driver, the weather is getting hot. Switch on the Air Condition, I'll pay, and I want some music, driver. Hey! You're driving too slowly for my liking. Speed up."

A melodious, gospel music poured from the speakers. Joe shouted. "Driver, stop that gospel music. It's not Sunday and I'm not in church. Go to 77.9 FM for some heavy rap." Quickly, the driver obeyed, and Joe began to nod and tap his foot. "Is there no fuel in the car, driver? Speed and overtake all these wretched cars in front of us."

The driver throttled a bit until they arrived at the hotel, then Joe went to the restaurant and sat in the corner. "Hey! Waiter!" he shouted, "I'm tired of English breakfast. I want a continental breakfast." Joe smiled and crossed his legs.

Joe viewed the Atlantic Ocean, the whitish sand on the beach and the swaying coconut trees whilst he was eating. Then he began to think of how to spend the money.

He first thought of his mother, Auntie Christy, who sold fruits at the market. For years, she had struggled to look after the four children. She was a single mother who single-handedly ran the house. It would be good to give her mother some of the money, but he had to tell her the source of the money because Auntie Christy was a devout Christian and if she knew of the source, she would hand him over to the police or force him to send the money back.

Gradually, Joe settled on an idea. He would tell his mother that the money was from a pen friend in Europe. He made the calculations and decided on the amount to give her. Then he thought of his younger sister Sally whose picture he used and called her Lucy. He would buy some clothes for her and then pay her school fees.

As he took the last swig of the tea, he smiled and whispered to himself because he had heard of people bragging that they had taken English breakfast or Continental breakfast, and thought it was something very special. He vowed to tell his friends that he was the first to eat a continental breakfast.

Suddenly Bigboy called, but Joe refused to pick the call because he remembered the promise he had made to Bigboy. When the call was persistent Joe switched off the phone.

From the hotel, Joe went to Oxford Street to buy four pairs of jeans, two mobile phones, T-shirts and four pairs of designer shoes. He even bought some perfume and gold chains for a girl he was wooing. The excitement of impulse-buying gripped him as he moved from shop to shop buying more things until Bigboy called again. Reluctantly, Joe picked the call. "Yes, BB. What's up?" he said in a shivering voice.

"Where are you, Joe? You promised we'll chill today after cashing the money."

"I'm sorry, I'm home. I'm down with malaria."

"Sorry to hear this. I was waiting for your call for us to paint the town red."

"There's a problem with the money. Smith didn't send it."

"Maybe he has seen that you're tricking him."

"I'm drowsy in bed now, will call you tomorrow."

"Don't worry. See you later."

Joe chuckled after the call. He ordered the taxi driver to take him to the shopping mall to have his lunch. At table, Joe felt big as he ordered waiters who doted on him.

When Joe was tired of shopping that day he decided to go home. At the back of the taxi, he ate ice-cream whilst listening to reggae music and yelling at the driver to overtake other vehicles.

Bigboy was very sad his friend was down with malaria so immediately after the call he did not hesitate to buy some fruits, yoghurt and biscuits and headed to Joe's home. Surprisingly, the first person he met was Sally, the person Joe used for his deal. "I want to see your brother Joe who is down with malaria."

Sally was taken aback. "Who told you Joe is not well? Joe is very fit. This morning he was in high spirits and told me he was going to town and that he would make me happy when he returns because his pen friend in America has sent him some money."

Bigboy felt dizzy as if the earth was dissolving around him but with courage, he picked his phone and called Joe again. "Joe, how is the malaria?"

"It's getting worse. I was rushed to the clinic and given some drips. I'm still weak in bed."

"OK. I wish you a speedy recovery."

Bigboy and Sally chatted heartily, and occasionally he would steal glances at her. Bigboy felt pity for Sally because her picture was used to swindle people.

As soon as the taxi stopped in front of the house, Joe, in good spirits, carried his heavy shopping bags towards the house. He was humming a song and was not aware Bigboy was leaning against a pillar. "Sally! Sally!" he screamed, "today is more than Christmas. We're going to celebrate with a big party. Sally! It's been shopping after shopping till I nearly dropped dead. The cash is in, Sally. I'm a cash man. Just look at my wallet…"

"Good afternoon, Joe, malaria boy…" Bigboy's voice boomed.

"BB! My God---" Joe trembled, and the shopping bags dropped from his hands. Bigboy grinned at Joe. "I came to visit you as a good friend. I brought you these things to help you get well soon. Take them, I'm off."

Joe's jaws hung loose. He stammered, "Er—er---please---er—BB---er---let me explain--- er--- Oh! ---er--- things to you---."

"Joe, I need no explanations from you. You're weak in bed so keep on treating your malaria. I've parted ways with a selfish guy like you." Then turning to Sally,

Bigboy whispered, “Sally, you have to be careful of your brother.”

“What has my brother, done, BB?”

“Just be careful.”

Tears hatched on Bigboy’s face as he left the house. He stopped occasionally to muse. How could Joe treat him like that after he had spent a lot of money on him? Bigboy’s mind recalled the various food joints and cinemas they had attended, the clothes he bought for Joe. He took his handkerchief and dabbed the tears on his face.

14

HAPPINESS

Genevieve's phone rang but the voice at the other end was strange and mumbling. Genevieve listened attentively for some seconds and realised it was Jim, the old man Esi had invited. "How are you, Jim? What can I do for you?"

"I want to see you as soon as possible."

"Any problem?"

"Please, I want to see you."

"Where's Esi?"

Jim burst into tears and told Genevieve that he had been abandoned for the past days and that anytime he called Esi, her phone was off. Genevieve tried to call Esi, but the voice prompt said the phone had been switched off.

The next moment, Genevieve was on her way to meet Jim at the hotel. She was shocked Jim looked frail and his skin was badly tanned because of the fierce tropical sun.

"Your friend Esi has swindled me to the tune of five thousand dollars. I'm not bothered by that at all. I want to discuss a secret with you. I don't want to mince words to take your precious time. When I set my eyes on you that day, I just had a change of mind..."

"I don't understand you, Jim."

"Please wait till I finish."

"In fact, the first day we met, I fell in love with you. I felt more attracted to you and have been thinking of you since."

"Are you serious, Jim?"

"I'm serious and I'm prepared to do everything in this world to make you happy. If you accept my proposal, I'll be the happiest person in this world. Please consider my request."

"It'll be serious to take over from my friend, Esi. How can you fall in love like that?"

"It's really and truly love at first sight. You have occupied my mind since."

"I'm sorry Jim. It takes time for people to fall in love. I've met you once and yet to know you. Moreover, you're in this country because of my friend, Esi. You don't even know my background; I don't know you."

Jim smiled for the first time and his leathery face looked like a mask. "I'm a retired civil engineer from the Netherlands. I'm divorced and I have two children who are working in the Middle East. After my divorce I became a lonely man and so I decided to sell my property and live in Africa. I want to take up citizenship here and enjoy the last days."

Genevieve looked at his tanned face once more. The wrinkles on his face were like little rivers overflowing with the tropical sweat. His protruded forehead was like a leaning mountain carrying a nose which jutted out clearly. Suddenly, Genevieve felt a cold, wet, palm clasping her palm. She looked at the drenched, hairy hand which did not send a ripple in her. The clammy hand gripped her tighter but still Genevieve did not feel any blood rushing through her; it was as if she was holding a dry stick.

The tears which mixed with the sweat on the masked face of Jim were frightening. Quickly, Genevieve pulled her hand and stared at him. For the first time she saw the bluish cat-like eyes dimming into his head. He had no eyebrows so one did not know whether he could blink. Then Genevieve looked at his ears which were stuck to his head like satellite dishes. At once, Genevieve feared Jim.

"Just accept my proposal and I'll give you all that you need. I'm prepared to buy a house and a car for you. Think about it."

"I must go now, Jim."

"Won't you give me assurance?"

"I've not decided. I'll think about it."

As Genevieve left, she felt as if she had been caught in a web. Her zigzag steps drew her into the web of the giant spider Jim who was enticing her to enter and be seized. But Genevieve was very cautious and was at the fringes of the web.

It was when Genevieve arrived home in the evening that she felt the spider seizing her. The offer from Jim was too attractive to ignore. Thus, it was not strange when Genevieve woke up several times in the night to think of the offer. By midnight she had resolved to accept Jim's proposal. She imagined the new house. The cars rolled before her until she settled on a Toyota Highlander. The next moment she thought of a sleek, black, Mercedes Benz car. Then her mind roamed the boutiques on Oxford Street, and the Mall. Genevieve was riding on the cloud of glory throughout the night until the cock crowed at dawn.

Another idea began to clear her earlier choice. Jim was too old and frail for her liking. She could not imagine being in the company of a man who was cold and lifeless and did not stir her emotions in any way. Genevieve sat on the bed and whispered, "Is life only about money, cars, and houses?" She shook her head in the dark. Genevieve got up and stood by the window. The wind blew the curtains, revealing the full, yellow moon. Genevieve looked at the moon brightening the dark sky. She was excited about the moon and gazed at it and whispered. "I like you moon. You are bright and happy. I want to be like you and be happy in life. Happiness is a good thing? I want to be happy."

Genevieve began to meditate more on happiness. Can one be happy when one does not like a person?

At once the thoughts of Bigboy came to her. There was something in Bigboy which attracted her, but she could not explain. Genevieve saw the bright moon receding into the clouds. Gradually the brightness faded when the dark cloud swallowed the moon. Suddenly, Genevieve resolved finally not to accept Jim's offer. She picked her phone and typed the message: I'M SORRY I DON'T THINK I'LL FALL IN LOVE WITH A GUY LIKE YOU. In anger, she pressed the "SEND" icon several times until the phone went blank. Her heart begun to beat faster when she realised, she should not have done that. She dropped the phone then heaved a deep sigh.

* * *

Joe wore his new jeans and the oversized T shirt which had the bold inscription: CHICAGO BOMBERS. Whistling, he sprayed expensive perfume on his clothes, wore the Nike boots and placed the groove of the sunshade on his nose. Next, he looked in the mirror, admired himself, took some hasty dancing steps and pushed the bulged wallet into his back pocket. Joe called Emelia, his new girlfriend, to accompany him to watch a new film which would be premiered at the cinema.

Unexpectedly, Joe's mother knocked on the door. "Joe, a gentleman from the Criminal Investigations Department wants to interview you." Immediately, huge bubbles of sweat hatched on Joe's face, his legs could not carry him any longer. He held the doorpost firmly. "Mum, I'll be with him soon."

"Are you sure you're not wanted for an offence? I've taught you to speak the truth."

"No, I'm clean."

Joe felt the breeze from the window. In a flash, the deals he had engaged in reeled before him. His heart beat fast as he walked towards the window. Joe realised that the die was cast, so he dived through the window, crashed on the stones and ran frantically without looking back. His mother stood akimbo, wiped tears from her eyes and knelt to pray.

15
SEAGULL

The senior high school results had been released and it was the topmost news which gripped the city. The news was all over. Slim and Genevieve had been given admission to the medical school. Esi passed only two subjects and vowed not to continue with her education. Surprisingly, Esi had applied for a visa to travel to the United Kingdom for greener pastures. Mrs. Ansah, Esi's mother gambled the family fortune away, broke down mentally and was admitted at the psychiatric hospital.

The greatest among the guys and girls was Bigboy, who failed all the subjects! Suddenly, Bigboy felt deserted by his friends, who refused to pick his calls and always gave the excuse they were busy preparing to go to the university.

That dewy morning, Bigboy's mother returned drunk from the night club and heaped tons and tons of insults on him. She called Bigboy a fool and a thief who stole his father's money. Bigboy cried loudly, decided to flee the house, when he received a text message from Genevieve which troubled him. For months, Genevieve was his solace, and he had her picture on the wallpaper of his phone which he glanced at daily. Bigboy was fed up with home so in shoulder-shuddering sobs, he made his way towards the beach to take the final and the greatest decision of his life.

Bigboy perched on the hump of a cliff on the coast and as he cast his gaze around, he felt like a monarch surveying his kingdom. Far off were the horizon and the pale, blue, sky. There were no canoes on the sea because it was Tuesday, a day the fishermen rested.

Soon he felt the breeze from the Atlantic Ocean mop the sweat off his face. Deep, down, below him, was the stony beach. As the waves bashed the stones below, they left their foamy debris of seaweed and crabs in the sands.

Even though the scene was captivating, Bigboy carried the gloomy feeling of distress and grief in him. Suddenly, the wind combed the surface of the sea, rolled the waves that bashed the foot of the cliff, scattering showers of salty water towards the summit.

Bigboy removed the mobile phone from his pocket and read the strange text message a hundredth time. Since the message came, it had stoked the pain in him. Each letter of the message seemed to be mocking him. Bigboy read the message the last time: I'M SORRY I DON'TTHINK I'LL FALL IN LOVE WITH A GUY LIKE YOU.

Instantly, Bigboy's eyes were loaded with tears when he saw a strange, lonely, seagull flying from the horizon towards him. The bird cried harshly then wafted on the waves before dipping down gradually to pick something from the deep.

The incessant cry of the seagull mingled with the roaring waves became a song in his ears. Bigboy listened thoughtfully and heard the sea singing. Strangely, he enjoyed the song, smiled, and muttered, "Even the sea knows my plight and is singing for me."

Surprisingly, Bigboy did not see the seagull again. Then he started wondering what had happened to the bird. Did it drop into the waves willingly and drowned? The longer he thought of the mystery bird, the happier he became and wondered if he could also jump and dip himself into the waves.

The roaring waves were deafening, and the rising sun cast a rainbow over the bluish ocean. Bigboy could not look at the radiant rainbow; he blinked and cast his eyes down, waiting for the rays to recede.

Then suddenly, his thoughts rolled back into the past. For years he had thought that he was the only child of his parents. He was told that his father, Mr. Bosman, arrived in Ghana twenty-two years before and married his mother. Mr. Bosman had been a shrewd businessman who shuttled between Accra and the major cities in Europe. He had run his business at home and the family did not know the nature of what he sold. The money poured in and Bigboy, at a tender age, was able to open the safe and steal huge sums of money which he used to entertain his school mates. He had enjoyed that loot for years until the real character of his father began to unfold.

First was the arrival of a white lady called Jacqueline from the United Kingdom, who was legally married to Mr. Bosman. Her arrival created a conflict in the family which led Adwoa, Bigboy's mother, to leave the marital home.

Then more conflicts tore the family and a major legal tussle ensued; Jacqueline was able to secure custody of the children and the joint property abroad. But those episodes did not deter Mr. Bosman from going about his nefarious business activity. One day another disaster struck Mr. Bosman. On one of his trips to Europe, he was busted for drug-trafficking, and jailed for twenty years.

The news struck Bigboy to the core. His father's property was seized so they left the plush home to live in a one-bedroom flat. Bigboy had hardly recovered from the blow, then more disaster followed when he could not pass the high school examination to be admitted to the university.

Strangely, most of his friends who were from poor homes, who he fed, clothed, and gave money to, had gained admission to the university.

But the unkindest disaster of all was when he received the text message from Genevieve that she was not in love with a guy like him. For years, Genevieve had been the centrepiece of his life. His entire world was anchored on Genevieve and without her the world became an empty place. What even hurt him to the core of his heart was the new relationship he had heard was developing between Genevieve and Slim who were getting ready for the medical school.

Bigboy's mind travelled deeper into the past. He could picture Slim, the famished, shabby-looking boy he fed on fast food, clothed in Levi's jeans, taught how to sing, dance, and eat ice-cream. Slim, the boy from the slums, whose house they could not trace. Why should Slim be an ingrate to eat his food and snatch the only girl he loved in the world? At once, tears drooled from his eyes. Indeed, love had made his world come to a standstill. It looked like the universe was against Bigboy, and even his relationship with Joe had been torn apart since he experienced that selfishness and greed.

Bigboy stood akimbo on the cliff, thought of the mysterious seagull again. Then he felt he should be like the seagull. He would spread his arms like a bird, look at the far horizon, the waves, and the stony beach and take a deep plunge headlong, crash into the jagged stones below and wait for the waves to surge and carry him off into the abyss of the ocean. Bigboy was determined to do it.

Gently, he placed the mobile phone by his foot, outstretched his hands, and looked at the horizon. His heart twanged in his chest and bubbles of sweat burst on his face. He began to feel dizzy when he looked down. But Bigboy had resolved to do it.

He resolved to count to ten then take the headlong plunge to end it all and be free from a broken home, selfish and ungrateful friends, and shame Genevieve. Yes, his lifeless body would torture Genevieve forever.

Bigboy began the count: one… two… three… four…. then there was a strong breeze which nearly lifted him up.

The count continued: five… six… seven… and … eight…. he felt a little tremor under his feet. Nine…. then the mobile phone rang piercingly. Bigboy was so shaken that he knelt to pick the last call before ending it all. When he looked at the screen, he saw the number and the picture on the wallpaper and felt some warmth floating down his spine. The text message in the inbox read: SORRY THE TEXT MESSAGE WAS NOT MEANT FOR YOU. Bigboy smiled and heaved a sigh at the last call from the only girl he loved in the world – Genevieve!

DISCUSSION

In the story "The Sea is singing" we cover the following key themes:

1. Friendship
2. Peer pressure
3. Family life
4. Social media
5. Suicide

1. Friendship

Many of us keep friends who play big roles in our lives. In the story, "The Sea is Singing" we see types of friendship among the characters.

Let's discuss the following questions:

(i) Give two reasons why we keep friends.

(ii) In the story, comment on the type of friendship of Bigboy, Joe and Slim.

(iii) State briefly the friendship between Esi and Genevieve.

(iv) Discuss two causes of breakup of friendship.

2. Peer pressure

A (i) Have you come across the phrase, "peer pressure" before?

(ii) What does it mean in a relationship?

(iii) Did your understanding of "peer pressure" the same as the definition below?

Peer pressure is a feeling that one must do the same things as other people of one's age and social group in order to be liked or respected by them.

B. In "The Sea is Singing" there are many examples of peer pressure.

(i) Discuss two examples of peer pressure in the story.

(ii) Why do people easily accept pressure from their peers?

(iii) Have you ever been pressured by your peers? Narrate your experience.

(iv) Discuss two ways you can withstand peer pressure.

(v) If you were Slim, what reason would you give to convince Bigboy to save you from the ear piercing?

3. Family life

All of us are born into families. We are brought up in our families by our parents or foster parents. Families are not the same in character and behaviour. For example, we have many types of families such as rich families, poor families, strict families, responsible families, and irresponsible families. In the story, we come across different types of families. Let's discuss the following:

(i) What type of family is your family?
(ii) Discuss the family of Bigboy.
(iii) Write a short paragraph on the family of Slim.
(iv) Write a short note on the family of Esi.
(v) Give reasons why you like or dislike the role played by Mma in Slim's family?

4. Social Media

An effective means of communication these days is the social media which uses digital channels to share information. We have many types such as:

YouTube
Facebook

Twitter

Snapchat

TikTok etc.

(i) State two benefits of social media in our lives.

(ii) State two negative uses of social media.

(iii) How did Joe and Esi use the social media?

5. Suicide

Suicide is the act of intentionally causing one's own death. There are many factors which drive people to commit suicide. It is not a good thing to try or commit suicide. When you face problems in life, don't keep them only to yourself. Share your problems with your parents, siblings, trustworthy friends, pastors, teachers, and professional counsellors.

(i) In the story "The sea is singing" Bigboy nearly committed suicide. List at least three factors which drove him to make the attempt.

(ii) If you are the friend of Bigboy, how would you advise him NOT to attempt suicide again?

GLOSSARY

Banku – it is a Ghanaian dish made of slightly fermented cooked mixture of corn and cassava dough formed with single-serving balls.

Kebab – pieces of meat, spiced and grilled on a long, thin stick.

Kenkey – it is a Ghanaian dish made from fermented white corn.

Koko – it is a porridge made from corn, millet, or Guinea corn.

Koose – it is a spiced, fried bean cakes.

Tro-tro – privately owned mini buses that travel on specific routes. These vehicles can be boarded anywhere along the route.

Tuozafi – it is a maize or millet dish. It is eaten with a special green vegetable stew or soup.

Waakye - is a Ghanaian dish of cooked rice and beans.

Wele - processed cow hide served as meat.

www.ingramcontent.com/pod-product-compliance
Lightning Source LLC
LaVergne TN
LVHW041117150826

845673LV00007B/2094

* 9 7 8 9 9 8 8 3 4 1 3 8 1 *